The Woman Series

Finding LOVE AFTER 30

GET READY FOR THE MAN
GOD HAS FOR YOU

The Christian Professional
Woman Series

Finding
LOVE
AFTER 30

GET READY FOR THE MAN
GOD HAS FOR YOU

DR. NADINE VARGAS

Copyright © 2022 by Nadine Vargas, Ph.D.

All Rights Reserved. No portion of this book may be reproduced in any form without permission from the publisher, except as permitted by U.S. copyright law. For permissions, contact: nadine@nadinevargas.com

ISBN: 9798361645350

Imprint: Independently published

Cover Design: Tehsin Gul
Interior Formatting: Amit Dey

Unless otherwise indicated, all Scripture quotations are taken from the Holy Bible, New Living Translation, copyright © 1996, 2004, 2015 by Tyndale House Foundation. Used by permission of Tyndale House Publishers, Carol Stream, Illinois 60188. All rights reserved.

Scripture quotations marked (NIV) are taken from THE HOLY BIBLE, NEW INTERNATIONAL VERSION®. Copyright© 1973, 1978, 1984, 2011 by Biblica, Inc.™. Used by permission of Zondervan

Disclaimer: *Although I hold a Ph.D., and am an experienced teacher and a trained nurse, I am not your therapist or financial advisor. The information provided in or through this book is for educational and informational purposes only and intended solely as a self-help tool for your own use. Please note that I do not guarantee the results of the information applied in this book. I share educational and informational resources that are intended to help you succeed in life. You need to know that your ultimate success or failure will result from your own efforts, your particular situation, and innumerable circumstances beyond my knowledge and control.*

DEDICATION

For my beloved husband, Nelson.
Prince charming couldn't beat you!

CONTENTS

A Gift For You ix

Introduction xi

CHAPTER 1: Don't Focus on Your Pain; Focus on
Your Dream 1

CHAPTER 2 There is Nothing Wrong with You 11

CHAPTER 3 Know What You Are Looking For 19

CHAPTER 4 Become the Person You Would Like to Date . . . 29

CHAPTER 5 How to Get Blessed 41

CHAPTER 6 Waiting is An Active Process 51

CHAPTER 7 You Don't Get Your Way? Pray! 59

CHAPTER 8 Get Yourself Ready to Date 69

CHAPTER 9 What to Do When Nothing Works 79

CHAPTER 10 How to Find Mr. Right 91

You Can Help Your Sisters Find Love After 30 101

Your Next Steps 103

Acknowledgments 105

About the Author 107

A GIFT FOR YOU

Thank you for picking up a copy of my book. You're the reason I wrote it.

I'd love to send you a special gift. It's a free audio featuring **"The 7 Must-Haves in a Future Husband."** I'll also send you a beautifully-designed checklist of the "Must-Haves" to keep handy as a constant reminder *that you deserve the best.*

As a bonus, I've also recorded positive dating affirmations you can listen to anytime to stay encouraged and inspired as you get ready for the man God has for you.

Just visit: Gift.ChristiansFindingLoveAfter30.com

I can't wait to hear your love story.

Blessings,
Dr. Nadine

INTRODUCTION

No more stumbling in the dark; it's time to find the right direction!

There are a lot of professional Christian women in their thirties (and beyond) who are still single. Successful extraordinary ladies can't believe their private lives aren't as successful as their professional ones. They are disappointed, frustrated, disillusioned, sometimes even bitter or at least discouraged, and often at their wit's end.

"What am I doing wrong?" and *"How can I find my soulmate?"* are legitimate questions that must be answered.

I've gone through this process myself. I want to answer those questions for you, helping you understand your situation and inspiring you to take the right actions instead of hoping for better luck next time.

God doesn't just have a plan for your professional life. He also has a plan for your private life. Stop asking yourself the devastating question about whether it is God's will for you to be single, feeling alone and desperate. Marriage was HIS idea!

Jesus made it clear that he came to bring you life and life more abundantly (see John 10:10). No, he wasn't cynical, and it wasn't a figure of speech; he meant it! He didn't come to make you abundantly lonely or abundantly disappointed. His goal was to bring you overflow!

The world has changed, and relationships are not as stable as they have been in the past. Two hundred eighty-one million Americans have been going through the devastating experience of a divorce, both that of their parents or their own. An alarming divorce rate of 50 percent is holding steady here in the United States[1], raising the question of how to find Mr. Right —someone who is willing to stay in a relationship with you, even if he is not "right" all the time.

Making the right choice from the beginning can spare you the painful experience of a divorce later; a divorce is the last thing you want after a long search.

- To choose right from wrong, you need to have profound knowledge and clarity about the question of what you should be looking for.
- To have a choice, you need to become the woman God and your future husband want you to be.
- To find what you are looking for, you need the guidance of the one holding the world in his hand.

This book is here to help you act wisely, stop the passive waiting, bring clarity and knowledge into your thinking, and show

---

[1] Neil Clark Warren, Ph.D.: Date or Soulmate? (Nashville, Thomas Nelson, 2002), page 195.

you how to partner with God in your search. The approach presented in this book has been tested and tried. It is both spiritual and practical.

Don't look back one day with the nagging question: *What if I hadn't given up on finding love?* Don't waste one more day; time is precious! You are responsible for acting and moving toward the brighter future you've been dreaming of.

CHAPTER 1

DON'T FOCUS ON YOUR PAIN; FOCUS ON YOUR DREAM

This week was stressful and full of frustration. Your bipolar colleague was in one of her low phases, and your jealous competitor was in attack mode all week because you beat him by a mile on the last project. Non-stop cynical comments, a lack of willingness to cooperate, and, on top of that, the craziness of a colleague with a highly dysfunctional psyche. All this, coupled with an overwhelming amount of work every day.

Finally, the weekend rolls around. It is Friday night; the work week is over. This is supposed to be when the fun starts. Instead, the sound of silence screams at you the minute you walk into your apartment. As soon as you arrive home, you are painfully aware that nobody is there. *What will I do to relax and enjoy myself? Why did I work so hard all week long… and for who?*

You planned to go to a restaurant with your best friend, and you have been looking forward to it all week. Finally, someone will listen to you with an understanding ear, somebody you trust and have known for a long time, but now you are home alone, and the only creatures listening to you are your houseplants. A feeling of heaviness befalls you. Sadness and disappointment are gripping your chest, and your body sends stress signals into your system.

You take off your coat and head towards the kitchen with heavy steps. Your closest companions are sad and weary as you prepare a cup of tea to relax and comfort yourself. You sit at your living room table with a steaming hot cup of tea. The aroma of a proper brew is streaming into your nostrils.

Slowly you start to sip your tea while your gaze slides out the window. The sun hasn't set yet. There is still enough time to go running in the park. After all, you are not one to wallow in self-pity. So, you decide to escape your misery and do something useful with your time. While finishing your cup of tea, you take a deep breath, pull yourself together, and decide to go running.

Fresh air, a few last glimpses of the sunlight, and the refreshing effect of exercising help you fight your feelings of weariness and frustration. Squirrels are playing in the trees, and the birds are singing while you are making progress. It was a good decision to leave the house, not giving in to these feelings of defeat and disappointment, and running always helped you to stay in shape while it recharged your batteries and gave you a sense of accomplishment.

Thinking that, you are asking yourself: *"Wouldn't it be cool to run a Marathon? Why not work towards another goal? If others can do it, why shouldn't I be able to do it?"* It is one of those things you always admired in others but never considered doing yourself. Maybe now is a good time? You are still single and free to make your own decisions. What you do after work and on weekends is entirely up to you. Why don't you move towards a new dream?

And here is one of the keys. Don't focus on your misery, disappointment, frustration, fears, or pain; focus on your dreams!

When you focus on your problem and reflect on it constantly, you will lose vision and eventually drown in your own misery. Just remember the story of Peter in the New Testament, how Jesus called him out of the boat. As long as he kept focusing on Jesus, he did the impossible and walked on water just as Jesus did! But the moment he lost focus, he began to sink. What happened?

The water was still the same, Jesus was still the same, and they hadn't changed location either! Only one thing in the story changed: Peter's perspective. Instead of looking at Jesus, he looked at the waves and started to fear. As soon as fear arose in him, doubt polluted his perspective, faith declined, and Peter sank.

Don't allow that to happen. Find your dream and focus on it, knowing that Jesus is the author behind your dream. When he calls you out of the boat, you can trust that his helping hand will be there for you in times of doubt and weakness. Call out his name, just as Peter did, and he will meet you in the middle of your storm, no matter how high the waves are.

He sees you, he hears you, and he will never let you drown. It is not your responsibility to save yourself. Your job is to keep your focus, get your gaze back on the goal, and then take one step at a time. But before you can do that, you need to decide who you want to be and what you want to have accomplished when you meet Mr. Right.

Maybe you are thinking: "My biggest dream isn't running a marathon or writing a book; my biggest dream is to find Mr. Right!" Well, that is all right, and I firmly believe you shouldn't give up on your dream. But whatever we handle in life, we should take it with wisdom.

According to Ecclesiastes 3:1–8, everything in life has a season. We cannot determine the season, but we can determine what we do with our time during each season. Just imagine how odd it would be to decorate your house with Christmas decorations on Easter. Buying candles, shopping for a Christmas tree, wearing a winter hat and thick woolen gloves. Wouldn't that be totally out of season? Of course, it would!

So even if you wish for summer in winter or autumn during springtime, you will not be able to determine the season. What you can do is make the best out of every season, and this is what I strongly encourage you to do. If you decide to make the best out of every season, I can assure you that you will certainly not regret it. So instead of focusing on what you don't have, focus on what you can do now and then do it wholeheartedly.

Become the Best Version of Yourself

Give yourself permission to dream. Get a vision of the ideal version of yourself. What does the ideal you look like? What has your perfect self achieved? Who do you want to be when you meet your future dream man?

Find clear answers to those questions, and then get to work.

While I was waiting for my husband, I was doing precisely that. If it had been up to me, I would have met him much earlier in life. But looking back on my season of waiting, I must admit that I wouldn't have accomplished many things in my life if I could have determined the timing.

While waiting for my husband and preparing for him, I lived in three different countries, traveled a lot, made many international friends, and studied to become a nurse, a teacher, a PhD. in social sciences, and a doctor of letters in humanities. On top of that, I was writing books, fighting for human rights, building a house, taking care of my parents, and running a marathon, and I still fit the same size as I did when I was 20 years old.

No, I am not bragging here. I am telling you this because I want you to understand that if I could do those things, you can do them too! Needless to say, I didn't do anything in my strength. God was the one who strengthened me and to him goes all the glory. But while this may sound like an impressive list of accomplishments, these were not the most significant changes in my life.

The most significant changes in my life have taken place inside of me. I would never be the person I am today if God had not actively used my season of waiting to work on my personality. Patience, for example, is not one of the characteristics I was born with. But I had to learn how to exercise patience because I would never have willingly submitted to my husband, as the Bible says, had God not been working on my character.

But these inner changes were at least as significant as the outer successes, and they all contributed to my preparation. Therefore, I can only urge you to make your waiting time active and meaningful and become the best version of yourself while allowing God to work on your personality. The result will be fantastic!

Permit Yourself to Dream Big Dreams

Mary Kay Ash was famously quoted as saying:

> "There are three types of people in this world: those who make things happen, those who watch things happen, and those who wonder what happened."

We all have a choice. You can decide which type of person you want to be.

Many people have dreams for their lives but fail to make them a reality. If you want to see your dreams come to pass, you must be determined. An aggressively positive attitude will be needed to protect you from a passive, negative mindset that always leads to failure. Decide to be a person who will make things happen!

Have you ever heard of a negative thinker who lived an incredibly positive life? These components are contradictory to each other and cannot coexist. Negativity, or "stinking thinking," as Joyce Meyer put it in one of her sermons, is always destructive. I am convinced that negative thinking will always lead you to the pit and never to the top!

Since you are a believer, I cannot believe that God hasn't given you a dream for your life. Challenge yourself today and give some thought to the dreams that God has put into your heart. Forget about the nay-sayers who try to pull you down to their level. Don't be afraid of your past mistakes. We all make mistakes sometimes. There is no shame in falling; there is only shame in staying down.

So, dust yourself off and go back into the ring, life goes on, and the future is yours, child of God! Now write down your dream and start working toward it because:

"Dreams don't work before you do."

—John Maxwell

Keep the Vision in Front of Your Eyes

A teacher asked her sixth graders to write down their dream of what they wanted to be in life. In the class was a little boy named Steve from a low-income family. He was dressed in hand-me-down clothing and suffered from an embarrassing stuttering problem. Little Steve had seen a funny man on television who made people laugh. For Steve, it was clear that he wanted to become like this man, making people laugh.

On the day the paper was handed back to the students, little Steve was called forward, expecting to get complimented. Instead, he was asked to rewrite his essay and think about a realistic dream he could accomplish. In the evening, he shared his disappointing experience with his father.

His very wise father encouraged him to read that very same paper that described his dream, aloud every morning before school and every evening before bedtime, thanking God that his dream to be on TV making people laugh would come to pass. Little Steve did precisely that year after year. Today, Steve Harvey is on television every day, causing thousands of people to laugh.

Don't let anyone talk you out of your dreams. If you don't, you'll be the one having the last laugh!

CHAPTER 2

THERE IS NOTHING WRONG WITH YOU

Why Are You Still Single?

You probably never thought you would still be single. I know how you feel; I felt the same way. Doing everything by yourself is no fun. When you go to the shopping mall and watch other happy couples walking hand in hand while you are on your own, you feel the pain. You feel the pain when you feel alone and need somebody to comfort you.

It is painful not to know when this is coming to an end and not knowing what you will do on your holidays. Your married friends think you must have an awful lot of time on your hands because you can do everything you want any time you want to do it. They forget that you have nobody to send to the grocery store while cooking because you just saw that the milk is empty or that there are no eggs left.

They do not see that you have to carry your own suitcase when traveling, which hurts. Silently you ask yourself: *"What is wrong with me? Why can't I have what my friend Alisa has, a loving husband who carries the heavy suitcase for me when we are heading to the airport? What is wrong with me?"*

Plain and simple, there probably isn't anything wrong with you! None of us is perfect, of course. If you are looking for perfection in others, or even within yourself, you will always find something wrong that can be straightened out. Therefore, we need love and patience for ourselves and others.

Even the Bible encourages us to do exactly that: *"Love your neighbor as yourself"* (Matthew 22:39 NLT). So instead of beating yourself up and asking yourself what is wrong with you, please understand that there are a lot of attractive, intelligent, well-educated, professional, adorable, and even good-looking Christian single ladies out there. Do you think that there is anything wrong with them? Far from it!

My own sad experience is that the more you are committed to your walk with God, the more you work towards excellence in different areas of your life and character, the more difficult it becomes for you to find a quality match. The dating world is tough.

Pointing out this problem, Pointing out this problem, I must tell you the story of a unique person who became a christian. After finishing her university studies, she decided to do another degree, and moved to a different country. There she met a nice Christian man. He went to church, worked as a university professor, and, best of all, he liked her! He was great company, so they decided to deepen their friendship and started seeing each other. However, the enthusiasm didn't last long when she discovered that this man wanted to have sex with her.

She was shocked and disappointed because he claimed to be a Christian. This lady is not a compromiser, so they stopped seeing each other. See the point? There is nothing wrong with my friend! She is pretty, intelligent, funny, and well-traveled. Talking to her is fun. She will never run out of good stories or interesting topics. The problem? She isn't a compromiser; she is determined to do the right thing. Therefore, she suffers.

The world today is deeply polluted. Wrong ideas of what a relationship is have taken over. A lack of commitment and lack of mutual respect, paired with oversized egos, dominate many relationships. There is no longer even a consensus that sexuality should be relational.

Fast, non-binding satisfaction is desired. People want to have fun; responsibility does not fit into this concept. Sad to say, a lot of liberal ideas have invaded the church today, and there are a lot of compromisers in the Body of Christ. Ouch, that hurts! Even so, it is the truth, and if you don't want to compromise, you will probably feel the consequences sooner or later.

You are special, and you are looking for someone special. Give it the time it needs. You are looking for a treasure, not for a pebble.

You Are Precious

I have often made the mistake of finding my worth and value in being accepted by others. What others have said about me has determined my emotional world. Have you ever made this mistake? Don't get me wrong, we all want to be liked, loved, and accepted, and I am no exception. Still, the outside world shouldn't dictate our worth and value. When we are looking for a partner, we can easily fall into this trap.

I haven't found my better half, so I'm only worth half as much as others? This is nonsense! Our value is based on something, or rather someone else, and that is Jesus. He loves us and should be our first love. Your future partner will not save you; Jesus saved you and is lovingly at your side. You're not alone!

But Nadine, don't you understand? I need a human being to talk to! You are right. You and I need a human counterpart to exchange ideas, recharge your emotional batteries, and gain the kind of self-awareness that helps you become a better person. God knows this and provides for you in this regard as well. But when we make our self-worth dependent on another person, we give that person a degree of power over us and our emotional world that they don't deserve.

You are complete because you are totally accepted. You are complete because you are deeply loved by God the Father. You are complete because you are completely saved. You are complete because you belong completely to God's family.

Sometimes you feel isolated because you are single, and most church activities are focused on families and not on the needs of singles. Even the sermons are almost never tailored to your situation. I know you may not feel that way, but you are precious, loved, and important and belong to a big universal family, dear sister. Even if we haven't met in person, I'll tell you here and now that you are precious to me.

Get Your Hopes Up!

I know that many disappointments tend to leave us hopeless. Maybe your disappointment led you to the conviction that it is better not to be hopeful because that could lead to new disappointments, and you hate to feel disappointed! Well, we all do.

I have never heard of anyone who embraced disappointment with gusto. Possibly you think you are a hopeless case; after all, it went wrong several times. But that is not the truth.

Joyce Meyer once said that God has special grace for a special case. So, if you are a special case, what's the trouble? Get your hopes up!

Hope was my email password for many years, and I was delighted when my hopes became a reality. Hope is the force that broke the chains of Joseph. Hope is the force that helped Esther succeed in changing the destiny of her people. Hope and faith were the forces that filled the disciples with so much boldness that they changed the world forever, rocking the whole Roman empire. Hope is a powerful force that changed the world many times throughout history, and hope is the force that will change your world too.

There's a scene in *The Chronicles of Narnia* when the White Witch kills Aslan while spitting the poisonous words at him: "Despair and die!" That is exactly what the enemy wants! He wants to see you discouraged and disappointed, which eventually will lead you to hopelessness and despair.

Don't allow him to have his way. You're a fighter! A few setbacks cannot defeat you. Drive the devil to despair and take delight in the God of all hope. No season in life will last forever; get your hopes up!

> *"And this hope will not lead to disappointment. For we know how dearly God loves us, because he has given us the Holy Spirit to fill our hearts with his love."*

(Romans 5:5)

CHAPTER 3

KNOW WHAT YOU ARE LOOKING FOR

Know What You Really Want in a Man

For you, it is clear that you have been single long enough. Something must change; better sooner than later. But what exactly do you want to change? Of course, you don't want to feel excluded anymore from groups of married friends or church activities that are designed to serve the families in the church. You want to have a family yourself, of course, or at least a spouse to grow old with.

Often enough, you try to wrap your brain around the question of what you will do when your parents have passed away, and you can't celebrate Easter or Christmas with them anymore. I do understand that you are fed up with it because I was fed up with it too. Still, you must know exactly what you are looking for in a man who could be your future husband.

If you love to exercise and eat healthily and get married to a smoking couch potato who is munching a package of chips every evening while watching TV, you set yourself up for unhappiness. It may be true that opposites initially attract each other, but are they compatible over the long term? Certainly not when it comes to important values.

Of course, you can be the counterpart of your quiet husband, who prefers to listen rather than talk. Imagine both of you always like to talk; who would ever listen? That kind of "opposite" is okay. I am not talking about stuff like that. I am talking about core values and lifestyle. On top of that, you should find your partner attractive too; after all, you will look at him for the rest of your life. So better make sure you like what you see.

While I was waiting and looking for a partner, I made a very precise list of characteristics, beliefs, and qualities I was looking for in a man. Please do that, too, and know what you are looking for. On my list were items like:

- Loves the Lord first and then me.
- Looks good.
- Has a good education.
- He is smart.
- Likes to exercise.
- He is physically well-groomed.
- He is passionate and protective.
- Has a good heart.
- Has vision and entrepreneurial spirit.
- Has similar interests and hobbies.

Praise God for my husband, who has all these qualities.

I know you are fed up with being single, and I understand! But please don't make the mistake of compromising on core values, or you will regret it later. And don't tell yourself that you can fix him later. Nothing will change at the altar.

When a man takes you to the altar as a lazy man, he will be a lazy man at home. If there is a major problem with your potential future husband, don't decide for him. He doesn't want to change to get you? He will not change to keep you! An easy fix will not do, you have to find Mr. Right, and everyone else is simply wrong for you.

What Is a Good Choice?

A good couple is a couple that God will join together at the altar when they say yes to each other. Just make sure it is really God who joins you together because he is very picky and doesn't join everybody! Don't blame him for your divorce later; if he didn't join you together, you are blaming the wrong person.

Many couples who have been married in churches shouldn't have been there. They should have gone to the registration office downtown to get the job done there; they didn't even qualify to get married in a church. Why? Because the Bible says: "It is not good for the man to be alone. I will make a helper suitable for him" (Genesis 2:18 NIV). What man is God talking about?

To understand this verse, we have to read verse eight first, which is much less quoted but not less important. This verse tells us that God has planted that man into a garden in a place called Eden. In verse 15, we read that God had a purpose for this man: to work (cultivate, develop) and take care of the garden.

We also know from Genesis 3:8 that God was walking with Adam through the garden. What does that mean? It means that the man, Adam, lived in God's presence. He worked in the garden, named all the animals, etc., and cultivated the place, meaning he was responsible for that place. When God said it isn't God for man to be alone, he was talking about THIS man. So, who qualifies as a future husband?

- A man who lives in Eden (God's presence).
- A man who works.
- A man who acts responsibly.

For this man and this man only (!), it is not good to be alone. If he doesn't fulfill these criteria, don't take him. Being married to a lazy man is no marriage; it's a catastrophe! So, if the two of you are not in the garden, you don't qualify for marriage. Keep this one thing in mind: East of Eden isn't a good dating place! The two of you have to be in Eden, or all hell will break loose.

Don't make the mistake of going to church on Sunday, trying to find Mr. Right somewhere in the jungle on Monday while planning to drag him to church after marriage: *"Do not be yoked together with unbelievers. For what do righteousness and wickedness have in common? Or what fellowship can light have with darkness?"* (2 Corinthians 6:14 NIV).

Imagine a Shetland pony and an ox yoked together. That will cause the little pony much harm. Besides, you would be married to a dead man since the Bible says that people without God are spiritually dead. Do you really want to talk to a dead man for the rest of your life? Very creepy thought, isn't it? Again, if you are dating a man who is not in the garden and doesn't like to work, he doesn't qualify at all. Run from him while there is still time!

I saw in my own family that it doesn't work. One sister married a lazy man, and both of my sisters married unbelievers. The two of them changed dramatically in character, and not for the better.

As the Scriptures say, *"A man leaves his father and mother and is joined to his wife, and the two are united into one"* (Ephesians 5:31). Being one with a "dead man" is impossible. There will always be a division between the two of you.

But Nadine, what will I do if there is a really nice guy who wants to date me? Should I just say no?

For sure, the safest way is to say no. But I know about a famous Christian couple who successfully chose to risk getting to know each other better before he received Christ. The man was intrigued by the lady and sheepishly asked her: *"I probably have no chance of dating you, do I?"* She said, *"Not if you don't go to church with me."* He went and found Jesus.

Before you get enthusiastic, let me lovingly warn you: it takes a very strong personality and mindset to hold on to your faith. My sister tried to do the same with her future husband. He also went to church with her but stopped going the day after they married.

I know from a few love birds who went to church together. They ended up in bed with the guy, and the guy decided not to marry them after they slept with them for a while. There is nothing to gain in the enemy's camp. Only disappointment, a lack of fulfillment, and deception are to be found there.

So, if the guy doesn't prove his sincere faith for an extended period, there is no way you should even consider marrying him.

He hasn't genuinely changed if he wants to convince you to sin. He is not the one for you. A man in God's presence who is working and proves himself as a responsible person is the only man who meets your minimum standards. If he wants to convince you to sin, he hasn't truly changed. He is not the one for you.

What is a Good Match?

If you don't have enough matches, you do not match! Sounds funny and very simplistic, right? Looking closer at this point, you will realize that it is not as simple as it sounds. A lot of things have to be considered to make a good choice. The more you know about the critical points you must not forget when you start seeing someone, the easier it will be to decide whether you should continue seeing each other.

Dr. Neil C. Warren even states that the following points will help you make the right decision after just two dates. Similarities in a relationship are like money in the bank, while differences are like debts owed. Differences will be like open construction sites that require a huge amount of hard work, and this work will drain you of greatly needed energy to keep a marriage thriving. Making sure that the similarities are many and the differences are few will spare you a lot of pain, frustration, and disappointment.

The seven most significant similarities:[2]

1. Consensus about spiritual questions

Spiritual harmony is the most important similarity for any couple. You cannot live in harmony with somebody who doesn't share your Christian worldview. I am not referring to a common religious

---

[2] Neil Clark Warren, Ph.D.: Date or Soulmate? (Nashville, Thomas Nelson, 2002), page 115 – 128.

affiliation, although that is also sometimes important. I am referring to the more profound matter of spirituality that has to do with the larger context in which you view your life. Basically, the question revolves around your belief in a personal relationship with God and not just some god. Is Jesus Christ your Lord and Savior?

    2. The desire for verbal intimacy and ability for intimacy

True intimacy has the potential to lift you into the world of emotional oneness.

Intimacy requires sharing your deepest thoughts, feelings, dreams, fears, and longings. That requires you and your partner to be good at at least three things.

    a. An ability to connect with the other person.
    b. Clarity about your own needs and desires.
    c. Willingness to listen carefully.

These three ingredients result in a couple becoming what the Bible calls "one flesh" and the sense that their personalities melt into each other in a healthy way.

    3. A similar level of energy

Look for somebody who has about the same energy level as you. Men tend to have a little more energy for biological reasons. Be careful if there are signs of lethargy or depression.

    4. The same amount of ambition

If you are a person with little ambition or if you have much ambition, both will become obvious very soon. Are you content with a typical career and life, or are you shooting for the stars? If you are aiming high and have lofty dreams, you should look for somebody who is a go-getter, just like you. People with very different ambitions will have a painful relationship. It simply doesn't work when one pulls and pushes while the other constantly puts a foot on the brakes.

5. Similar perspective about roles

In Greek mythology, a creature with two heads is the synonym for an ugly monster. If both of you want to sit in the driver's seat, you surely will head toward an accident! Talk about your expectations concerning the different roles you have to play in marriage and come to an agreement before you say, "I do."

6. Common interests

Whatever we love to do, we love it even more if we can do it with somebody we enjoy spending time with. However, if every discussion about plans for the weekend leads to war within your four walls, you will not enjoy your spare time together.

7. Personal habits and behaviors

If you don't want to wake up next to a person with stinky breath, make sure that your future spouse is in the habit of brushing his teeth. Find out what habits you desire in your future husband and which ones you can't tolerate before it is too late.

I strongly recommend you use this proven checklist; you will benefit as much from it as my husband and I did.[3]

---

[3] Neil Clark Warren, Ph.D.: Date or Soulmate? (Nashville, Thomas Nelson, 2002), page 115 – 128.

CHAPTER 4

BECOME THE PERSON YOU WOULD LIKE TO DATE

Don't Mess Up the First Date; Nail the First Impression!

Don't kill the dating process before it starts, or it could be a lost opportunity. I am sure something similar has happened to you in the past too. But let me invite you into the situation. Imagine me sitting in a cozy little café in the old town area, surrounded by beautiful half-timbered houses, cobblestones, and tall, ancient trees. Sitting there, looking good and smelling great, I am waiting for my rendezvous.

To my embarrassment, I must admit that I have never been in the business of being massively early, but I also wasn't late, so I arrived in time, expecting the man who wanted to get to know me better to be there already.

However, he wasn't there. Five minutes went by while I was looking around, enjoying the atmosphere of the beautiful scenery around me. Another five minutes went by, and I started to wonder where the man was. Another five minutes passed when annoyance set in, and I considered leaving the place. Five more minutes went by as a relaxed man walked through the door, heading for my table.

Instead of a reasonable explanation, he had nothing to offer but a lousy excuse. Politeness was one of the key values instilled in us by our parents, and that's why I stayed polite, but only because of that. Upon closer inspection, it turned out that his fingernails were poorly trimmed and had dark edges. His clothes looked sloppy and badly ironed. So a good-looking, well-educated man suddenly seemed entirely unattractive to me. Before he could ask me to meet again, my answer was already set.

Another time I met a very well-educated, handsome, perfectly dressed, and athletic-looking guy who even was the president of an important engineering association. The man was Christian, he didn't live far away, and he was perfectly on time as we met at a beautiful spot beside a lake.

I like gardens and so did he, so we decided to visit a Chinese Garden that was very close. At the entrance, he showed no sign of wanting to pay the entrance fee for me, even though it was reduced to the equivalent of a dollar due to ongoing renovations. The cashier remarked, *"If I had such an attractive companion, I would pay the entrance fee for her."* His answer was, *"I'd rather pay the larger bills."*

After the visit, he wanted to go for a walk by the lake, even though the biting cold of January had already turned my hands blue, and I would have preferred to go to a cafe. He stretched out the walk as much as he liked because he felt like it. His comment was: *"I just feel like it now."*

When he finally started to freeze, he suggested going to the cafe of his choice because that's where he felt most comfortable. So that's where we went. When the waiter served the tea and wanted to collect the money right away, he had to make a quick phone call at that very moment. When he came back, he dominated the conversation for hours. Yes, you heard right: *for hours!* When I tried to politely excuse myself three or four times, he said every time:

"You can't go now. You have to stay. Anyway, I made extra time for this afternoon, and I'm enjoying our meeting right now." The situation culminated for me when he pulled a checklist out of his pocket and asked me aloud about my attributes and qualifications to make sure I was a lucrative match for him.

At the end of the day, I was completely blown away and never wanted to meet that person again. Even his long declarations of admiration and attempts at persuasion, which he stubbornly sent to me for days after my rejection, didn't help. I really didn't want to experience an afternoon like that again.

The bottom line is to try to behave in a manner that will lead to a positive first impression. Based on this first impression, the decision for or against further meetings will be made. Whatever you decide, you don't want to make an impression like this. As Christians, we must keep the Golden Rule in mind; we should treat others the way we want to be treated (see Matthew 7:12). Doing that, we are building a firm foundation for a good and long-lasting relationship.

Tips for your first date:

1. Safety first. If you don't know this man's background very well, make sure you meet in a public place and that someone knows where you are, in case the date is not going the way it should. Tell a friend to call you after the first hour. That gives you the opportunity to excuse yourself if the guy is boring. If things are going well, just don't answer the phone!

2. Dress to impress—and smell good—to nail the first impression. Choose an outfit that you like and feel

comfortable with. Something that seems to be tailored for you.

3. Be chatty but allow the other person to talk. Nobody wants to listen all the time.
4. Be humorous! You are nervous, and so is your date. A little joke here and there makes the conversation enjoyable, and the situation will be more relaxed.
5. Leave your mobile phone in your pocket and be present. If your mobile phone is more important to you than your conversation partner, you are showing a lack of interest, which is rude.
6. Smile! You don't have to smile nonstop but try to smile a lot. A man likes to be around a friendly woman. Nobody wants to go out with a grouch.
7. Be yourself, or you don't allow your dating partner to get to know YOU. Mr. Right will be interested in you for you, not the lady you are pretending to be.[4]

See how it is done? Don't tell me that you can't do that. If I could do it, you can do it too. I am cheering you on!

Keep the Fire Burning

Good, you did a great job. Your first date went well. You both had an enjoyable time and an interesting conversation. The guy wasn't rude. He wasn't late. He smelled good and was funny. For

---

[4] https://www.eharmony.com/dating-advice/getting-to-know/first-date-tips/, 10/25/2022

https://www.menshealth.com/sex-women/a19545021/first-date-tips-for-men/, 10/25/2022.

you, it is clear you want to see him again! But wait a minute, don't move forward too hastily.

Maybe it comes across as a little bit old-fashioned, but it gives him a chance to take the initiative to pursue you. Most men are hunters and don't like to be hunted—not if they have a genuine interest in you. They may feel flattered at first, but my suggestion is to leave the ball in their court. Yes, there may be a few exceptions of very shy, insecure men who need a little help. One text message might be acceptable, but a flurry of messages isn't going to help your case.

Let's assume you have been successful on your date, he is asking for permission to see you again, and you say yes. How do you build your relationship now? Let me give you a few universal pieces of advice to help you build a good and hopefully lasting relationship.

Most of the things you have paid attention to during the first date will continue to be important while you move forward in the dating process. What is changing now is the depth and quality of the relationship, and here are a few things to consider:

1. Now is the time to do a lot of things together. You want to experience your potential future husband in many ways and contexts. How does he act in his everyday life? What are his routines, and what are his reactions when he is challenged? These are things you must observe, and they will be very important later.
2. Remember to have a good time. Putting too much pressure on a new relationship is no good; you must allow this relationship to grow, or it can break.

3. Learn how to communicate. The time for small talk is over, you need to learn how to communicate, and that means listening actively. Make eye contact, stop doing other things and be aware of nonverbal signals as well as the spoken word. Make sure you ask questions to clarify whether you got the message right *"Am I right in thinking that you feel like...?"*

4. When you are talking about an issue, make "I" statements such as: *"I feel confused when you make statements like 'I love you,' and three days later you tell me that you don't know if you are ready for a deep relationship."*

5. Be respectful to your partner in every situation, even when you become familiar with each other. Respect is as important to a man as love is to you. Keep that in mind, always.

6. Discuss issues upfront. If you don't, they will grow or show up later.

7. Be willing to compromise; you can't have your way all the time.

8. Make your values known to your partner. Sharing the same values is very important or you will move in different directions. Do understand that it is impossible to sail the boat in two different directions at the same time. Try it, and you will see that one of you will go overboard.

9. Demonstrate honesty and build trust. Building trust means that you are trustworthy in being consistent in your actions and that you do what you say you will do. Break those rules, and you will see how doubt creeps

into your relationship.[5] Jesus said: *"Just say a simple, 'Yes, I will,' or 'No, I won't.' Anything beyond this is from the evil one"* (Matthew 5:37).

Seven Simple Ways to Become More Attractive

Here are seven simple things you can do that instantly make you more attractive:

1. Selflessness pays out

The Bible is true in every way, and it tells us that giving is better than receiving (see Acts 20:35). Why? A study has shown that helping others in a selfless way is more attractive than beauty when it comes to those looking for a serious, lasting relationship.[6]

2. Compliments work[7]

Though you might think that a man is so strong, cool, independent, or confident that he doesn't need to get compliments, that is wrong. Praise is crucial in any kind of romantic relationship – just make sure, that it is honest, heartfelt praise. He needs to hear that you appreciate him. Men love to get compliments too! The following compliments will make your potential date smile:

---

[5] https://www.wikihow.com/Build-a-Long-Lasting-Relationship#: 10/25.2022
[6] https://www.independent.co.uk/life-style/love-sex/attractive-how-to-look-more-men-women-simple-ways-red-clothes-hip-sway-a8295776.html, 10/25/2022.
[7] https://bestlifeonline.com/compliments-men-cant-resist/10/25/2022

"I love the way you think"
"You always know exactly what to say"
"Can you help me fix this?"
"You're a great listener"
"It's amazing how hard you work"

3. Look friendly at someone and smile[8]

According to scientific research, maintaining eye contact isn't only a flirting technique, but it makes you seem more attractive too. A friendly look together with a smile boosts your appeal the most.

4. Lady in red

Men tend to see women in red as more desirable and sexier.

5. Pepper up your step

I must admit that this sounds funny, and it is totally up to you if you want to do this. But research shows that you can double your allure by swinging your hips from one side to the other.

6. Simply nod your head

A study has shown that people can appear up to 40 percent more attractive if they are nodding their heads in a conversation. This simple sign of assurance makes people more likable, approachable, and, therefore, more attractive.

---

[8] https://www.independent.co.uk/life-style/love-sex/attractive-how-to-look-more-men-women-simple-ways-red-clothes-hip-sway-a8295776.html, 10/25/2022.

7. Adopt an attractive posture

A study found that having your arms and legs facing outwards rather than crossing or folding them is seen as more attractive. Expansive posture signals seem to come across as openness and self-confidence, which are often seen as attractive.

CHAPTER 5

HOW TO GET BLESSED

An Everlasting Principle That Will Work Until the End of Time

Have you ever brushed your teeth with Colgate toothpaste, or do you know anybody who has never heard of Colgate? As a kid, I loved Colgate toothpaste because of its fresh taste. Today I moved away from it because my teeth have become a little bit more sensitive, and I need to use a product that hardens my enamel. But that's not what I want to talk about with you today.

My mission today is to inaugurate you into an old secret that worked for many people, past and present. A secret that made small people prominent and poor people wealthy. A secret that helped visionaries to achieve their goals and dreams. A secret that turned impossibilities into possibilities. A secret that will work forever and ever, and that secret is that givers gain: *"As long as the earth remains, there will be planting and harvest, cold and heat, summer and winter, day and night"* (Genesis 8:22).

Givers gain. Moving to New York at the age of 16, William Colgate told the captain of the boat that he wanted to get into the business of making soap. Listening closely, the captain advised him that if he wanted to become not only the biggest but also the best soap manufacturer, to do one thing consistently, *"Begin to tithe on everything that you receive."*

William followed the captain's advice, always tithing even more than ten percent of all of his earnings. He founded the

William Colgate-Palmolive Company, which became famous throughout the world.

John D. Rockefeller donated over five hundred million dollars to charity while walking this planet, and his name became truly great. Every year, thousands of people stand awestruck at the Rockefeller Center in New York around Christmas time in great admiration of the beautiful Christmas tree.

But neither of these great men invented giving. They simply put an important biblical principle to work in their lives:

> *"'Bring all the tithes into the storehouse so there will be enough food in my Temple. If you do,' says the Lord of Heaven's Armies, 'will open the windows of heaven for you. I will pour out a blessing so great you won't have enough room to take it in! Try it! Put me to the test!'"* (Malachi 3:10)

Did you know that this is the first and only time that God says we are allowed to test him? There is no other statement like this to be found in the whole scripture, underlined with three exclamation marks. Those exclamation marks show us with absolute clarity that God made this statement with strong feelings. He meant it, try him and you will taste and see that he honors his Word. Always!

But Nadine, I am not looking for an increase in finances. I am looking for a spouse.

First of all, some part of you probably *does* wish for financial freedom. Of course, that is not the point. Your primary goal is to find a spouse, and that's why you are reading this book.

No worries, I'm not trying to change the subject because I ran out of ideas. I only wanted to make a point. The promise of this passage is not limited to financial wealth; it's a general principle we can apply to many areas of our lives, including dating.

So let's get a little bit more specific here. Going back to the text, we see that the key statement is not about financial wealth. It is much broader. The key word here is BLESSINGS.

Isn't it a tremendous blessing to find true love?

> *"Place me like a seal over your heart,*
> *like a seal on your arm.*
> *For love is as strong as death,*
> *its jealousy as enduring as the grave.*
> *Love flashes like fire,*
> *the brightest kind of flame.*
> *Many waters cannot quench love,*
> *nor can rivers drown it.*
> *If a man tried to buy love*
> *with all his wealth,*
> *his offer would be utterly scorned."* (Song of Songs 8:7)

Love is priceless, precious, and strong. It's a true blessing as wonderful as great riches. Again, givers gain! There are many ways to give, and the tithe is one way to give and, in my opinion, the most important one. Not because I see it as such, but because God sees it as such. He even accuses those who fail to tithe of robbing him (see Malachi 3:8-18). Do you really want to rob God? I sure don't! He is worthy of all our love, and we all need his blessings.

I heard John Hagee say that *the tithe is not a dept we owe but a seed we sow*. Sowing seed into good ground always leads to a harvest. Jesus had a reason when he chose as an example an increase of thirty, sixty, and even a hundredfold (see Mark 4:8).

Sow and see your blessings grow! Payday is coming, and the harvest is always, always, always bigger than the seed you have been sowing!

But there's always a warning here. God says in Malachi 3:9 that, if you do not tithe, you are cursed with a curse. That's why you simply can't afford *not* to tithe.

There are many ways to give and sow. My suggestion is to sow towards your dream. *"Don't be misled—you cannot mock the justice of God. You will always harvest what you plant"* (Galatians 6:7).

Jerry Savelle, a famous televangelist who started out as a mechanic working on cars, told a story about seed sowing that became one of my favorite examples of purposeful giving. One day he went to see a friend who worked a farm in the southern states of America. His friend had been planting the same seed for many years. Consequently, he was reaping the same harvest for all those years.

One day Jerry traveled in a little airplane to see his friend. As he flew over the land his friend was cultivating, he was very surprised. All those years, his friend had been planting the same seed, but this time he saw something different growing there. Once he landed, he asked his friend: *"Didn't you plant cotton this year?"* His friend looked at him and casually said, *"No."* Jerry continued the conversation: *"But all these years, you have been planting cotton."* *"That's right,"* his friend answered, walking on. *"But why is it that you didn't plant any cotton this year?"* Jerry asked. The short answer was: *"Because I didn't want any."*

So, what are you going to do now? Right! You plant today what you wish to harvest tomorrow.

If you plant apples, you will harvest apples; if you plant potatoes, you harvest potatoes; if you are friendly, you will harvest friendships; and if you sow love, you will reap love.

Sow into Somebody Else's Dream

One thing I don't like about the "seed time and harvest" principle is that the word time is between the words seed and harvest. To make it very clear again, there is the seed, TIME, and harvest. Everybody who is into gardening or farming knows that principle. Nobody who ever grew anything in the garden or out in the field expected to harvest the day after planting seed.

What that means in the spiritual realm is that you have to take care of your seed while you are awaiting the harvest. What does that look like? For one thing, it means you have to water your seed with your confessions of faith and keep it safe from hungry snails or other harmful things such as unforgiveness, doubt, discouragement, or fear because they will suffocate the seed and kill your harvest. Get aggressive about it and immediately uproot everything that could harm your seed. The minute a little weed pops up, kill it!

Aside from that, wait expectantly for the harvest. Why do I point out that you need to do more than just wait, but that you have to take care of the seed and wait expectantly? Well, of course, because you want the seed to grow. So, make sure to protect the seed with your prayers and believe in your harvest, even if nothing is to be seen yet.

A lack of faith will lead you to give up on your seed and never reap your harvest. Don't let that happen, you have a right to harvest from your seed, don't abandon the seed, and I am sure your bumper crop of blessings is coming.

A few years ago, when my husband found the Lord, he made the decision to find a wife who was a fellow believer. Living in the world for many years, he did and saw a lot of things that he didn't wish to repeat or experience again. For this reason, he decided to wait for the woman God would bring into his life, even if it would cost him.

Without being fully aware of what he was doing, he started to do the right thing and planted a seed. My husband is a go-getter and a high achiever. At the age of 18, he joined the United States Marine Corps, became one of the few and the proud, and learned how to find the courage to fight and the will to win.

After he left the Marine Corps as a Lance Corporal at the age of 22, he went into the banking business and put into practice what he had learned as a Marine, to fight and to win. Turning 26, he already managed two branches for his bank in New York at the same time and won numerous awards and honors.

Looking for the love of his life, he convinced two church members to join him in founding a singles group. By doing that, he invested in other people's dreams. What started out with just five people eventually grew to about 25 believing singles who were actively pursuing their dreams.

One after another left the group because they started dating or lost interest. But he still couldn't find what he was looking for. However, two years later, he got to know me. Although I was never part of that group, and the circumstances were all against us, he realized quite quickly that I was the woman he was looking for and vice versa. In the end, he was the first member of the singles group to get married. And the first person who partnered with him in starting the group recently got engaged and will soon be married.

In my case, it took a little bit longer than that. For many years, I had to pray for others, volunteer at their weddings, and help to prepare for their weddings. When my friends got married, I cheered for them. When some of my friends got sad and frustrated with their singleness, I listened to them, and I prayed, prayed, and prayed some more for them to find their better half. Most of them got married before I did. Knowing what I know today, I would probably have sown a more precise seed into that dream, like starting a singles group or something similar, but back then, I just didn't know any better.

But the waiting paid off, and God's answer was even more amazing and mind-blowing than I could have imagined. My dreams came true, just like in a modern fairytale, and I do believe that God wants to do the same for you!

> *"Never give in. Never give in. Never, never, never, never—in nothing, great or small, large or petty."*
> —Sir Winston Churchill

CHAPTER 6

WAITING IS AN ACTIVE PROCESS

> *"Patience is not the ability to wait but how you act while you are waiting."*
>
> —Joyce Meyer

Make Waiting Delicious!

Do you sometimes find yourself in the situation of having to go shopping right after work?

Actually, you would like to go straight home because you feel tired and exhausted, but you remember, while driving, that you don't have anything left in the fridge. Your stomach tells you loud and clear how it's doing, and the biting hunger signals make you almost weak, so you head for the nearest supermarket. With quick steps, you rush through the shelves to get the desired groceries.

As soon as they are found, you head straight for the checkout. But what is that? It can't be true. There are no cashiers at most of the registers, and a huge queue has formed at the only occupied cash register. Frightened, you stare at the queue, and you almost drop your groceries. Taking a deep breath, you join the queue, full of disappointment, and the waiting begins.

After 20 minutes, you finally leave the supermarket. Whoever looks into your face now can read that you are not in the best mood. Annoyed, you drop your groceries on the back seat of your car. Exhausted, it's time to finish the drive home. It's rush hour, and the streets are full of cars. Almost every traffic light forces you to stop because a long queue of cars is already waiting in front of you.

Who cares? You are only two miles from home. Soon you will be able to let yourself drop onto the coach, and the relaxing evening can start. But suddenly, you hear a loud beep. You wince when you look at the car dashboard. Taking a closer look, you see the red symbol of a gas pump, which flashes at you as a warning signal. The tank is empty!

Completely unnerved, you head for the next gas station, which, fortunately, is on the route to your house. Just as you turn the corner and the gas station comes into view, you can already see what's happening here. A long line of cars has already formed at the gas station. Nobody will fill up the tank quickly now; waiting is the order of the day again. As far as you are concerned, the evening is over.

When I allow my instincts to take over, I find myself standing in front of the microwave, screaming at the instant popcorn: *"Hurry up!!!"* I don't know if you are as bad as I am or how far your patience is developed. But personally, I don't enjoy waiting much. In fact, I really don't like it.

In love with the term's effectiveness and efficiency, with a high drive to be productive, wasting time is among my biggest enemies. It always leaves me with the nasty feeling that all this beautiful time is wasted, wasted for good. You probably feel the same way. Waiting is hard because we feel that we have wasted our precious time. And you are right, because time is precious!

We all know that we can't turn back time. However, exactly at this point, the problem turns into a solution. Why? Very simple. Waiting doesn't have to be a waste of time. If we use our time of waiting wisely, the hours of waiting can become our finest hours. Isn't that great? As soon as we understand Joyce Meyers's quote that patience means understanding how to act while we are waiting, we take the lemons that life is throwing at us and convert them to refreshing lemonade.

Stop wasting your time and start to wait actively! Fill your life according to the season you are in right now with active waiting, and make your time of waiting count.

Take the Lesson, Do the Trip

Before you can find your partner, you should have found yourself. Not knowing who you are is dangerous; it blocks a healthy vision of what you are looking for. Getting to know yourself better is only possible if you experience yourself in different contexts. Here's a good motto to live by: Discover the world and find yourself!

What is wrong with trying out a few different lifestyles in a few different countries before settling down with conviction and without regret? Enjoy the journey and stop being anxious about where you are; you will get to the destination that's meant for you. Every deviation and shortcut is there for a good reason; no time is wasted at all: *"The Lord directs the steps of the godly. He delights in every detail of their lives"* (Psalm 37:23). Pray the following prayer on a regular basis. Ask God to reveal his will for your life to you, and be assured that God will never lead you in the wrong direction!

Prayer for Guidance:

Lord, you have a plan and purpose for my life. All my ways are known to you. Just as your Word says, you let me catch my breath so I can refresh myself, sending me in the right direction. For your own good reputation, you have delivered and saved me. To your own glory, you lead me in a life of excellence.

In your leadership, I have confidence, and I do not rely on my own understanding. In all my ways, I acknowledge you, trusting that you will direct my path.

The wisdom of the world means nothing to me, and I don't waste my time in the company of sinners or hang around with good-for-nothing people. Instead, I keep myself busy meditating on your Word by day and by night. Like a tree planted by the river, I am always fruitful, and everything I put my hands to turns into a great success.

The ways that you have for me are just perfect; I don't even have to be upset or wrap my brain around the question of what will happen to me in the future. For you are much smarter than me, and your ways are nothing short of perfect. Your goodness and blessings will continue to hunt me down for the rest of my life, and I will stay and live in your presence until the end of eternity.

Thank you that your Word is bulletin-proof no matter what and fit for every kind of stress test. It shines as bright as a lamp in the darkness to my feet and brightens up my path. I know that you enjoy watching me because I praise and glorify your name with the greatest awe and sense of respect. My self-confidence is rooted in your lovingkindness and mercy. Wherever I turn, You are my navigator that leads me safely to the right destination.

When I ask you for wisdom, you are never stingy. You never lose sight of me. Instead, you coach me and give me good advice along the way, and this is why I don't lose my way. God, you are simply the greatest; I am awestruck by the glory of your majestic name. Because of you, I haven't been falling flat on my face; without you, I would have lost my balance a long time ago.

Thank you, Jesus, for dressing me in robes of righteousness that allow me to come into the presence of the Father. Without your help, it would have been impossible. But with your help, everything is possible. I love you, Jesus, I do! Amen.

Discover the World

Discover the world deliberately, without fear or anxiety. Only entrust your way to the Lord, ask him to help you to be at the right place at the right time, and keep on moving, exploring yourself and the world, and experiencing yourself in different contexts. Nobody knows better than you what you always wanted to do.

Personally, I can truly state, that I never regretted the mindset of making my single life an adventure. Especially in times of harsh reality, when I was painfully aware of the fact that I still hadn't found what I was looking for, those adventures helped me look on the bright side of life.

Horse riding in Ireland, England, Iceland, and Spain, with or without my friends, was a wonderful experience. I've enjoyed amazing hiking adventures in the mystical Scottish Highlands, the German Alps, the Swiss Alps, and the Austrian Alps. I went skiing on glaciers and very high mountains in different countries and experienced a winter wonderland. Kayaking in the Czech Republic on the River Moldova and the German Danube was so beautiful and unforgettable forget. Cruising the Mediterranean Sea on a luxurious cruise ship and exploring a new city or country every other day was the experience of a lifetime.

Living on the Riviera in Italy and the international city of Zurich, Switzerland, allowed me to dive into new cultures on a deep level and opened up new horizons for me. There have been so many things that I have seen and done in those days of being single that I can simply not list them all here, and you probably don't even want to know!

But I cherish those experiences and have no regrets. Whenever I had a dinner party in my former apartment in Zurich, Switzerland, surrounded by my international friends, we had so many things to talk about that we never had enough time for all the stories we wanted to tell and experiences we had to share.

As a bonus, if you lead an interesting life, you transform yourself into an interesting person, and that can never hurt. The only thing I can tell you is that you should take the lesson and make the trip, there is no need to waste even one more day!

CHAPTER 7

YOU DON'T GET YOUR WAY? PRAY!

Dare to Ask Big

Televangelist Jerry Savelle blessed the people of Africa wonderfully with his ministry. They have built medical clinics and orphanages, trained pastors, dug water wells for widows, and many other things. Oral Roberts, one of Jerry's heroes, had heard about the many things he did in Africa and decided to give him a ring, asking for permission to travel with him next time. Floored and honored, Jerry agreed.

With great expectations and all excited, he traveled to Africa together with Oral Roberts.

The first point on their agenda was to open a medical clinic in Kenya. the President of the country was among the political representatives. All the dignitaries, politicians, and guests of honor, including Jerry and Oral Roberts, were gathered on a podium behind the President as he delivered his speech.

Knowing cameras were trained on the podium, Mr. Roberts began scribbling on a napkin. He pushed the napkin towards Jerry and asked him to read the scribbling. He whispered in Mr. Robert's ear, *"I can't read that."* Oral Roberts asked him to read it again, but he couldn't decipher it. *"What does that mean?"* Jerry finally asked. *"That means Oral Roberts"* spelled backward. *"Why is Oral Roberts spelled backward?"* Jerry asked. *"Because I'm bored by your small plans,"* Roberts replied.

That may have been an insult to the event planners…but what a compliment to God!

When you pray, does God scribble the letters DOG (God spelled backward) on a napkin because your little plans bore him?

The way we pray reveals a lot about us. When we ask for small, safe things in prayer, we show that we have little faith in God. Not just in his capacity to do everything he wants to do, but also in his love, goodwill, generosity, and trustworthiness. Sometimes we are deceived because we have been exposed to wrong teaching, which has sent us down the drain of religious thinking, such as: *"I don't deserve that much, God will not give me what I am asking for anyway."* Or you are asking yourself if it is in God's will to give you what you are asking for.

Actually, we have made prayer way too complicated. If we ask God according to his will, he will give it to us, and if we are not sure about what God wants, we simply have to read the Bible. The Bible is a reflection of God's heart and will, so we don't have to stumble around wondering what we are allowed to ask for or not.

Of course, God will not give you a married man because you fell in love with him and asked for him in prayer. That would be a selfish, sinful prayer: *"And even when you ask, you don't get it because your motives are all wrong—you want only what will give you pleasure"* (James 4:3). But if you ask him for a good man, a godly man with whom you will bring glory to His name, then you can include whatever comes into your mind after the characteristic godly. You can simply ask for everything! You have not because you ask not (see James 4:3).

Here's how John 16:24 puts it: *"You haven't done this before. Ask, using my name, and you will receive, and you will have abundant joy."* Abundant joy means lots of joy, overflowing joy. A joy that will make you look crazy because it will cause you to jump around! A joy that will make you laugh and wonder how all this is possible. *O really? Why is it that I have prayed for a partner and haven't received him yet?*

Even if it is not what you want to hear, the answer is: Ask and keep on asking. Knock and keep on knocking. Nowhere in the text can we read something like: Ask, and you will receive immediately, knock, and the door will open right away. Maybe sometimes, but certainly not always. Derek Prince, a former Professor at King's College in Cambridge, once shared an experience with the Lord while preaching. Brother Prince studied the story of Moses and asked the Lord, *"Why is it that Moses had to be prepared 40 years in the desert of Median, taking care of his father in laws sheep?"* Almost immediately, he could hear God whispering into his spirit: *"Because I couldn't do it in 39."*

Before you get hysterical thinking that you will have to wait for 40 years, let me comfort you. God knows how much time you have, and probably you won't have to lead a whole nation through the desert without a compass or map. So don't panic! God is not in the business of being early, but he doesn't come late either.

The key is to keep on asking Him in Jesus' name. Throughout the Bible, God tells us one hundred times to ask or request Him for things. One hundred times!!! Knowing that, you should really understand what you are supposed to do. Not asking is neglecting your duty of taking responsibility for your destiny. God can't be clearer. If we don't believe him after 100 times of repetition, we will not believe him after 1000 times of repetition.[9] So please do yourself a favor and ask!

A few years ago, I was very active in the fight against human trafficking and forced prostitution. While in London, I attended the year-end service of Pastor Nicky Gumbel, who has become famous as the author of the Alpha Course. After an inspiring sermon, prayer was offered. I had the idea of writing something on a research level on human trafficking and forced prostitution, and since I couldn't think of any better institutions in Europe than Oxford and Cambridge, I prayed with a prayer warrior for an open door to Oxford or Cambridge. Shortly after that, she remembered that she knew someone who was also involved in this matter, and I already had contact.

A few weeks and months passed when I suddenly received an enthusiastic e-mail from Cambridge asking me to get in touch if I was still interested. A short time later, I had the opportunity to join an international team of researchers, to work on a significant European study. I was invited to a symposium at St Catharine's College, Cambridge University, and later to the British Parliament to discuss the contents of the study with Lord Bernard H. Howe and Maria Miller, Minister for Women and Equality, among others. What a difference prayer makes!

---

[9] Terri Savelle Foy: ASK BIG. (Terry Savelle Foy Ministries, 2021) page 9.

Team Up for Success

> *"Dominion over every problem that you have begins with two in agreement in Jesus's name."*
>
> —John Hagee

No matter where you are in life concerning your finances, career, health, relationships, emotional health, business, or any other area of your life, two believers coming into an agreement can move more together than two million in disagreement. King Solomon, the wisest man who ever walked the earth, said this: *"Two people are better off than one, for they can help each other succeed"* (Ecclesiastes 4:9).

That verse often pops into my mind when my husband and I are doing something together, and it is very important to me to pray with him, every day, even when time is short. Why? Because I know that God's mathematical laws are different.

In the book of Deuteronomy 32:30, we read that one can chase a thousand and two can chase ten thousand to flight. Logic would say that if one can chase a thousand, two can chase two thousand. Not so in God's mathematical system. In God's mathematical system, two in agreement are heading toward a "quantum leap" that leads to a spiritual explosion that unleashes great quantities of supernatural power.[10] Think about an atomic explosion, and you will get the picture:

---

[10] John Hagee: Absolute Power. (Goose Creek Publishing, 2021), page 190-191

> *"I also tell you this: If two of you agree here on earth concerning anything you ask, my Father in heaven will do it for you. For where two or three gather together as my followers, I am there among them."* (Matthew 18:19)

So what can you ask for? ANYTHING!

Make up your mind today to find a person of faith, who comes into agreement with you, and then pray together, knowing that every prayer will hit that wall of resistance until it breaks.

Plan Your Time and Journal Your Prayers

> *"Early to bed and early to rise makes a man healthy, wealthy, and wise."*
>
> —Benjamin Franklin

How do you start your day?

I can imagine how stressful your life is. As a professional woman, your everyday life is hard work driven by a tight routine, and your job demands a lot from you. At this point, we are exactly on the same page. That's why I developed a morning routine years ago that puts prayer and meditation at the beginning of the day, accompanied by a good cup of tea.

Since no voice from the kitchen calls out the loving words, *"Darling, your coffee is ready!"* You'll have to find another way to warm up, at least temporarily. Maybe that sounds heartless! No, I really don't mean it like that; quite the opposite. Your single life should lead you into deeper intimacy with God, and the closer you get to God, the closer your dream man gets to you. It is important for God to remain your God; he does not want to lose his place in your life to a man. Therefore, invest in your relationship with him today, even if you have to get up one hour earlier, so he can prepare you for the relationship with your future Prince Charming.

I haven't felt prepared for my day without prayer for a long time, simply because I know what everyday life can throw at me. Preparation is everything. If we intend to be successful, we cannot afford to leave the house naked. Instead, we have to wrap God's promises around ourselves like a beautiful garment. However you start your day, pray!

Journal your prayers and see how God will work on them step by step. Journaling helps you keep your dreams in front of your eyes, and once your prayers have been answered, you can tell everyone how God transformed your mess into a message and your test into a testimony.

Many women are leaving the house without breakfast; coffee or tea will do it for the first couple of hours, we think. While I can agree with that, I still recommend feeding your spirit with the Word before you walk out the door to face the world.

Prayer for a Spouse

Here is an example prayer for your future spouse:

> *Lord, I know that you have only good plans for me. Plans to take care of me, not letting me down ever, and that allows me to hope and believe that my future will be bright. You are my light, and because you have only*

stored up good things for my life, I feel at peace and at ease.

I place my hope and trust in you, knowing that it will not be wasted. This man you have picked out for me will leave his mother and father exactly at the right time to be joined to me as one. Prepare me for him and him for me so that our relationship will be strong and fulfilling.

Thank you for never letting me down, in Jesus' name, amen.

CHAPTER 8.

GET YOURSELF READY TO DATE

The Importance of Emotional Health

"My friends are really annoying me; they are nothing but disappointing. Too bad I can't replace all of my colleagues at work either; they are nothing but annoying. At least I can avoid my parents! They are the worst of all; they will see nothing of me until next Christmas! Hopefully, God will give me a spouse very soon, so I don't have to bear with difficult relationships in the future anymore!"

Is that you? Probably it's not as bad, but if all your current relationships are problematic and your friendships never last longer than two or three years, watch out. You are on the way to divorce as soon as you get married, and if your face is looking like a reprint of the Book of Lamentations, you will most likely never get there.

Seriously. Only people who are capable of building long-lasting friendships and relationships are able to build healthy relationships with their spouses. *Well, that is different*, you say, *I am able to choose my spouse, and we will love each other*. But you are also able to choose your friends, and if you can't love them, what makes you think you will be able to love your spouse? In fact, you can't.

Preparation is everything. Nobody can run a marathon without solid preparation and training. What makes us believe that we can survive a marriage without preparation or training? Marathons and marriages have one thing in common; they demand endurance! See to it that you are equipped with the necessary characteristics and habits before you throw yourself into marriage, bringing yourself and somebody else into big trouble.

Don't get me wrong. I don't try to be discouraging or negative. My goal for you is to be aware of the pitfalls and the characteristics you need before you make the most important decision of your life (well, it's actually the *second* most important—after accepting Jesus).

Before I go into the topic of how to build stable relationships with others, I want to point out the problems that will stand against the positive development of a relationship. Dr. Neil Clark Warren, who has counseled thousands of married couples, states that most marriage problems are not marriage problems at all; they are emotional problems.

One or both partners brought deep emotional problems into their marriage, and when those problems arise in the newly-formed bond or even doubled there because both brought them, the marriage goes sour. Both individuals have to get well emotionally before they get married, because the marriage will never be healthier than the emotional health of the least healthy partner.

Many people are so deeply wounded emotionally that they should not even think about getting married. Wait until you are healthy emotionally, and then wait until you find somebody who is emotionally well, too; after that, you can get married.

"But isn't everybody a little bit unhealthy emotionally?"

"Absolutely NO!" We all have our weaknesses, and we can always improve, but that is not the same. [11]

---

[11] Neil Clark Warren, Ph.D.: Date or Soulmate? (Nashville, Thomas Nelson), page 99-101.

Enemies of Emotional Health

You can only feel good about yourself when you're emotionally healthy. People who lack emotional health tend to mistreat themselves and everyone around them.

The first step to finding out if somebody has an emotional health issue is observing your conversation. Healthy communication patterns lead to a flowing conversation, in which both people are talking, listening, and staying on the subject while showing respect for what the other person is saying.[12]

Anxiety in your partner or yourself shows through the following signs:

- a hard time looking you in the eye while talking
- never initiating a conversation
- seldom responding to your comments
- not following the general line of your discussion

Lack of self-confidence in your partner or yourself is showing through the following signs:

- aren't sure of their worth and therefore dominating the conversation as a mechanism of self-defense
- doesn't stop talking

---

[12] Neil Clark Warren, Ph.D.: Date or Soulmate? (Nashville, Thomas Nelson), page 99-101.

The severe disorder of narcissism shows in the following behavior:

- only talks about himself
- doesn't ask you anything about yourself
- the narcissist must be the center of attention; it is all about him all the time
- doesn't show any interest in your opinions or interests

If you notice any of the above behaviors, run! Narcissism is a highly-developed form of selfishness, self-importance, and self-love on a perverted level. Such people can only make others unhappy, even if they come across as very attractive and even charming in their own way.

If you see any of these signs of narcissism in yourself, go and get some serious counseling. You will never be able to build a healthy relationship. You have to understand that narcissism is not just a disorder, but it is a sin. Personally, I do not believe that a narcissist will ever change unless he finds Christ, repents, and wants to change from the bottom of his heart. And be sure he shows very serious signs of genuine change before continuing the relationship.

Poor communication patterns like the ones above lead to certain problems in a relationship and show that the person who has them is not ready for marriage. Such significant communication problems are only the visible signs of a more serious, deep-rooted emotional issue.

That doesn't mean somebody disqualifies for marriage forever; it simply means that there is some work ahead of this person or yourself.

Some degree of nervousness on a first date is normal. No nervousness at all isn't normal, either. But if there are continuing significant communication problems throughout the first and second dates, I would recommend stopping the dating process; something here is really wrong.

Beware of Character Disorders

Character disorders are very dangerous because they are a result of an underdeveloped conscience. If the church were a perfect place, you wouldn't find any Christians with such a disorder. Ideally, you will never run into anyone with a character disorder who claims to be a Christian. But this isn't an ideal world; it's the real world. And character disorders are not uncommon in the pews. You should also be aware that the devil sometimes goes to church, too.[13]

These are the signs:

- present themselves in a very engaging and reassuring manner
- super-charming
- say what you want to hear
- never differentiate from your opinion
- tremendously flattering
- tend to tell sweet little lies
- tend to exaggerate

---

[13] Neil Clark Warren, Ph.D.: Date or Soulmate? (Nashville, Thomas Nelson), pages 101 – 106

The person with a character disorder does all of those things because he is trying to reach a goal. Soon you will feel so lulled that you will find yourself sharing your most tender and intimate feelings, exposing yourself to particular danger. If the person can't reach his goal, he is ready to strike and hurt your feelings significantly. It means nothing to him to manipulate for his purposes. This person will cheat, lie and take advantage of others.

These changes will come very suddenly and often unexpectedly, because of an underdeveloped conscience;[14] someone with a personality disorder almost never changes unless a miracle happens. My suggestion to you is to protect yourself and stop the dating process today! As a Christian, you have the duty to love yourself as much as your neighbor (see Matthew 22:39).

Exposing yourself knowingly to such unhealthy influences is a violation of that law.

Any kind of neuroses—including depression—can be worked out and treated effectively. But the time to do so is before you are heading towards serious dating. Addictions of any kind are a highly dangerous and unpredictable risk to take. Active addictions of any kind are an absolute no-go and will lead to a failed relationship.

If you date a man who is eager to have a drink and another and even another, be very careful. Or if your date wants to have an alcoholic drink everywhere you go together, you are

---

[14] Neil Clark Warren, Ph.D.: Date or Soulmate? (Nashville, Thomas Nelson), pages 99-101.

dating a man with a drinking problem. No matter what kind of addiction it is, sexual addiction, eating disorder, pornography, jealousy, or anything else. The bottom line is that you or your date have to be emotionally healthy BEFORE you start the dating process.

The Way to Emotional Health

Unconditional love and authenticity are essential for emotional health. The source of unconditional love is God, and there is nothing that can change his love for you. A relationship with the author of love connects you with the ultimate well of love. Rooted in that love, you will find the courage to be your authentic self.

Some people abuse that principle. They are rude and moody to others, claiming that they are having a right to be themselves. That is a perversion of what it means. What it means is that I have the freedom to say what I truly like, dislike, think, need, wish for, hope for, fear, or even hate as long as I do so in love.

As long as you don't feel free to do so, you are bound to feel driven to please others. Don't get me wrong, the well-being of others, especially your future partner, should be highly important to you. But if you have to wear a mask to please them, you are not in the right company.

Likewise, you want to be connected to a man who has arrived at this place of true liberty as well. Prisoners are not happy campers and whoever enslaves himself to the opinion of the outside world is a prisoner of other people's opinions. Set yourself free if necessary and start living.

Characteristics of an Emotionally Healthy, Good Person

We have talked enough about emotional problems now. Let's move on and reflect briefly on the qualities that indicate emotional health and good character in a person.[15]

1. A good person will express attitudes of love, care, and unselfishness; your wishes and opinions count for them. Their love will show in acts of love and kindness. In a crisis, you can count on their loyalty according to the motto, *"A friend in need is a friend indeed."* They will speak up for you when somebody accuses you, and support you in times of trouble. An emotionally healthy person of good character gives time, energy, things, and emotions freely.

2. A good and emotionally healthy person is honest. Not brutally honest, but lovingly honest. Sweet little lies are still lies. Truthfulness is a good thing, and the love of truth is at the core of emotional health.

3. A good and emotionally healthy person is kind. Seventeen cross-cultural studies have shown that kindness is always among the top two virtues we desire in others. That is overwhelmingly significant.

Be of good courage, if you found a man with those qualities, especially if he has the must-haves and is free of all the can't-stands on your list. Provided you also meet the above criteria, you can assume that you are at the beginning of a promising relationship!

---

[15] Neil Clark Warren, Ph.D.: Date or Soulmate? (Nashville, Thomas Nelson), page 108-111.

CHAPTER 9

WHAT TO DO WHEN NOTHING WORKS

How to Accelerate Your Prayer Answer

1. Worship and praise

What could be nicer in summer than a small BBQ? The weather is perfect, you've invited some friends over, salads are made, and the table is set. Now all you have to do is light the coals so the meat can go on the grill, and you're good to go. You take some paper, cardboard, and matches and do your best, but the charcoal stubbornly resists burning.

After about 10 minutes, the box of matches is empty. Nothing's more annoying than that when you're about to start grilling. What now? If the coals don't glow properly, there's nothing to eat. Sure, a fire accelerator is needed! Half a bottle from last year is still in the garage. You squirt the fire accelerator onto the charcoal from a safe distance, and flames shoot up into the air.

From now on, nothing can go wrong; the coal is glowing.

Sometimes you feel that nothing is moving forward in your spiritual life. You pray, trust, and believe, but you cannot see any changes at all. Frustrating, isn't it? Desperation is creeping in. *What if God never answers? Maybe his answer for me is no, which is why he isn't saying anything.*

I know how that feels; it almost drove me crazy at times. *What did I do wrong? What have I missed? Why wasn't there any answer?* Those nagging questions drove me deeper into the Word, and

I wanted to get answers! What I have discovered, I will share with you. After all, I am here to take your hand, guiding you through the process. It starts with one simple verse:

> *"Enter his gates with thanksgiving; go into his courts with praise. Give thanks to him and praise his name."* (Psalm 100:4)

When you feel that you are sitting in a dark place, worship, praise, and thanksgiving may not come easy. It is as if the words are stuck in your mouth…or in your heart. Don't be discouraged, I felt the same when I started practicing worship, praise, and thanksgiving.

It just doesn't seem natural to praise when you feel like crying. Sometimes I think I did both at the same time, but I did it, and I kept on doing it, and I do it to this day. Why? Because God is good, and he deserves all our admiration and praise. But on top of that, it is a powerful weapon that opposes the world of darkness with all its evil opposition.

When we praise God in the midst of our impossible-looking situations, we move into God's presence. We praise ourselves forward. And where God is present, there is his power. One of my favorite stories in the Bible is the one about Paul and Silas in the dungeon. Read about it in Acts 16:25 and see how you get encouraged!

The story tells us that Paul and Silas were called to Macedonia by the Spirit of God. Following the calling, they went there and served the people, preaching the Gospel. Trouble arose when Paul got terribly annoyed by a slave girl, who was possessed by a demon spirit who followed them around, shouting right into Paul's ears. She made her master a lot of money as a fortune teller under the influence of this spirit. Paul rebuked the spirit, and it came out of her.

When the master of the slave girl learned what had happened, he got very upset. His hope for an easy income was gone. So Paul and Silas were grabbed and dragged before the authorities in the marketplace. This was nothing new for Paul. Angry mobs gathered around him quite often. Bringing up false accusations, the mob informed the officials that Paul and Silas were teaching things that were illegal for Romans.

The two of them were stripped naked and severely beaten with rods, then thrown into prison. Orders were given to the jailor to make very sure that they could not escape. So he threw them into the inner dungeon and bound their necks and feet to a block. Chained like this, they would have been hardly able to move.

When midnight approached, they did what nobody thought would be possible. They started singing, praising God in their darkest hour! They sang loud enough for the other prisoners to hear, bringing honor to God's name as a result. The two of them didn't care what anyone else thought; if the rest of the prisoners thought they were crazy, it didn't matter to them. They kept on praising the Lord in the midst of their impossible situation.

What happened next is truly mind-boggling. The text says the prison walls SUDDENLY started shaking, the doors opened, and the iron chains fell off! That is not fiction; that is in the Bible!

The story of Paul and Silas teaches us a real lesson. No matter how hopeless your situation may look, no matter how much you are hurt, no matter how deep the darkness is, no matter how thick the walls are, and no matter how often the doors are locked. Praise, praise, praise, and see how suddenly God will come onto the scene to set you free.

Do you feel like you are in a prison of loneliness? Praise, praise, and praise some more! God is always the same, yesterday, today, and forever. He changes not! Not now, not ever. Praise!

Not long ago, I was in a real crisis and had no idea how to get out of it. I began praising and thanking God for a full hour each morning. About six weeks later, the situation began to take a dramatic turn and was almost completely resolved. There are still a few things I have to wait for, but the whole situation has become much more comfortable since then, and I have complete faith in God that he will do the rest as well. In the meantime, I keep on praising and confessing, knowing that God is faithful.

When you praise, the world around you may or may not change, but the world inside of you will definitely change. Praise shifts our focus. We don't stare at the problem anymore; we look up to God, our solution. Doing that, our soul will be refreshed, meaning our mind, will and emotions will be more at ease. When you practice praise, you will discover how hard it is to praise God and stay depressed at the same time. He is worth a thousand Hallelujahs: *"Let the praises of God be in their mouths, and a sharp sword in their hands"* (Psalm 149:6).

Do you like being a victim? A victim of your circumstances, situations, impossibilities, etc.? Probably not. The minute you start praising, you are moving out of the position of a victim, into the position of a fighter. Darkness may surround you, but you are attacking this darkness with the sharp sword of praise. God's Word is like a sword, the sword of the Spirit (see Ephesians 6:17).

A sword is a weapon fit for offense and defense. Whatever the situation may be, the sword will help you to defend yourself and to attack. Wield the truth of God's Word against the darkness, and it will not be without effect. Worship is a sharp sword. So if you want to use an extra strong weapon, use the weapon of praise and fear not. Praise brings you into the presence of God; fear activates the devil and blocks your faith.

2. The Power of Thankfulness

In Luke's Gospel, the 17th chapter, we find the story about ten leapers who have been healed by Jesus. First, they asked him, and he had mercy on them and healed all of them. Sadly only one came back to say thank you, one alone. Jesus was obviously disappointed and asked the Samaritan who came back where the other nine were. He couldn't answer him. The next passage in this chapter is remarkable: *"And Jesus said to the man, 'Stand up and go. Your faith has healed you'"* (Luke 17:19).

If he was healed already, why does it has to be mentioned that he was whole? Very simple. The others have been healed, meaning that leprosy has stopped destroying them. But the thankful Samaritan got whole, meaning fully restored. The nose that was falling off from leprosy grew back; whatever leprosy had destroyed in his body was restored that minute. He was completely whole again.

Be thankful to God and say so if you want him to restore your life. Sometimes I feel that the enemy has stolen some of my life's good (younger) years and filled them with lack and attacks. No reason to get bitter! Even for my lost years, God has a solution:

> *"The Lord says, 'I will give you back what you lost to the swarming locusts, the hopping locusts, the stripping locusts, and the cutting locusts'"* (Joel 2:25). This is one of the reasons I, again and again, thank the Lord that he will bring back anything the locusts have eaten.

There is nothing that he cannot or will not restore. As for me, I have made up my mind that the enemy will keep nothing that he has stolen from me. My years will be fully restored; praise God!

3. Skip your plate

Whenever people wanted to find God's open ear throughout the Bible, they chose to fast. Not just in the Old Testament but also in the New Testament. King David fasted, Jesus fasted, and the Apostle Paul fasted, just to name a very few fasting heroes of the Bible. There are many ways to fast and reasons why we should. The Apostle Paul and King David both fasted when they felt distressed and wanted the Lord to act.

Daniel the prophet was in the middle of a fast, seeking answers for three weeks straight, when he heard from God:

> *"Then he said, 'Don't be afraid, Daniel. Since the first day you began to pray for understanding and to humble*

yourself before your God, your request has been heard in heaven. I have come in answer to your prayer. But for twenty-one days the spirit prince of the kingdom of Persia blocked my way. Then Michael, one of the archangels, came to help me, and I left him there with the spirit prince of the kingdom of Persia.'" (Daniel 10:2-13)

Actually, I don't like to fill my books with extended lines of scripture, as I do believe that you can read your own Bible. But in this particular case, I have to use one or two lines more, because I really want you to understand the concept. Daniel was fasting three weeks before he got his answer. Why? Because there was very strong evil resistance from the kingdom of darkness that blocked the answer.

When two devoted Christians are getting married, a powerful union comes into existence. The enemy surely doesn't like that and causes serious resistance. When Daniel prayed to God, he was heard immediately. But the angel that God sent to bring the answer to Daniel was mightily opposed by the spirit prince of Persia.

In the following verses, we can even read that the spirit prince of the kingdom of Greece opposed him too. Not just Daniel, but also the Apostle Paul taught us that we are fighting against those spirit beings from the kingdom of darkness (see Ephesians 6:12). From Jesus himself, we know that some of those spirits are so strong, that we can only get them in check with fasting and prayer (see Mark 9:29).

Our Christian life is not always a walk through the shopping mall; it includes fighting as well.

In the winter and springtime of 2019, I felt greatly convicted that I should give myself to fasting and prayer. In the autumn of 2018, I read a book about fasting by Derek Prince and felt greatly motivated to try it myself. During winter, I set one or two days per week aside to fast and had nothing but water for 32 hours. Between March and April, I gave myself to a partial fast of three weeks, only eating fruits, salads, and drinking water. No nuts or anything substantial. I wanted God to move on my behalf to send a godly husband into my life and took the matter seriously.

After at least two weeks, I think I got very brave and maybe even a little bit crazy in my prayers. At this time, I was still living in Zurich, Switzerland, in a beautiful apartment next to the park. Standing there in the corner of my living room, facing the dinner table, something came over me that made me pray a very bold prayer. I said:

> *Dear Father God, nothing is impossible for you. What is it to you to send me a godly husband? Because you can do anything, I ask you to send me a godly, attractive, good-looking man, who is very fit and loves to exercise and keep fit, just like me. A businessman, so that we can complement each other with our gifts, as I am not good with numbers. He cannot be older than three years, by the most, or he will be too lame for me and get on my nerves. Should he be a little older than me, he has to be even a bit fitter than me, or I will not be able to look up to him as a man.*

On top of that, he has to be intelligent too. Wherever he is now in the world, I do not know, but I ask you to prepare him for me right now. Do something in his life that will prepare him to be just right for me, and after that, bring us together. You have all the opportunities to do so. And if you want to do it perfectly, let him be from New England in the USA.

My husband, who is three years and three days older than me, a businessman and former Marine (fit!) from Connecticut in New England, told me in April this year that he had a severe crisis in April 2019. A total breakdown that left him so weak and desperate that he started to cry out to the Lord like never before. Shortly after, he found Jesus, got baptized in his name, and left his worldly lifestyle behind to follow Jesus.

Is there anything too wonderful for God?

CHAPTER 10

HOW TO FIND MR. RIGHT

God Can Only Navigate a Sailing Ship

Just a couple of days ago, I was invited to a lovely garden party for women. Talking to the guests, I found a lot of single ladies among the women. We talked about my book project, and all of them found it very interesting because they were single themselves or because they had a friend who was still single, also well above the age of 30. One thing that seemed to be particularly stressful for the women was that they didn't know how to find somebody.

"Where shall we look? Most couples in the church are already married."

That is true. Once you have passed the age of 30, you will find that most churchgoers around you are already married. But do you really look for somebody? Searching is an active process; we cannot expect to stumble accidentally over a box full of treasure. This is why treasure hunters go to certain places if they want to find something special. To find what you are looking for just by accident is very unlikely.

If we want to find something, we have to look for it. *"Ask, and it will be given to you; seek and you will find; knock, and the door will be opened to you"* (Matthew 7:7). It is not just a spiritual law but also simple common sense that you have to seek if you want to find. But how do you ever expect to find if you do not really seek? Or, as Joyce Meyer once said in a women's conference: *"You can't drive a parked car."*

Sailing in the Right Waters

Where are you looking for a husband, or are you actively engaged in looking for somebody at all?

A few weeks ago, one of my dearest friends, a professor from Los Angeles, who is a devoted Christian, took me totally by surprise. As we talked about her dating life, she said:

> *"Most men just take it very easy with their beliefs these days. They no longer want to know anything about commitment or waiting, or they take their relationship with God very lightly. Recently I actually spoke to a nice doctor who pointed out that a living relationship with Jesus in a potential future partner was important to him."*

That encouraged her. As we continued our conversation, I asked more casually: *"Which dating platform are you registered with?"* To my huge surprise, she gave me the name of a random platform. *"Are they even Christian?"* was my surprised question. *"No, not really,"* was her startling reply. *"But what do you expect then? When you go shopping, would you also look for cucumbers in the banana aisle?"* After a short pause for thought, the answer came: *"Yeah, right, I've never thought about that."*

Just imagine the following scenario. You go to a travel agency because you want to book a cruise. The travel agent asks you where exactly you want to go. *"Hmmm, I'm not quite sure yet. But I definitely want to soak up some sun and see palm trees. I've always been drawn to the south. I love beautiful sandy beaches with palm trees, and I've always liked being in beautiful cultural places. Perhaps you have a nice tour in your offer?"*

The travel agent types on her keyboard, stares at her computer, scrolls the screen up and down and says: *"Here we have something for you; I think this is just right for you. How about a trip to the North Pole?"*

As ridiculous as that sounds, the message is clear. If I'm looking for sandy beaches, palm trees, and southern towns, I can't travel north. I have to sail in the right waters to find what I'm looking for.

When I was looking for my husband, I tried to get very clear about what I was looking for. You know that I have had my prayer list already, but it was about time to extend it a little bit. I went back to Germany to build a house for myself and one for my parents that serves their needs perfectly, now that they are old. Being back in an environment that was actually way too narrow for me now, I came to the painful realization that I couldn't find anybody who would match my personality there.

I already had a list of characteristics that I wanted to have in a husband, but I wanted to be even more specific. So I said to God: *"Please let me find a dating platform with international Christian singles."* I had attended an international Protestant church called IPC in Zurich, and I truly missed the international environment that I had walked in for so many years. Searching Google, I found such a platform and wasn't that impressed. Most of the matches disappointed me.

Then one evening, as I was looking through my matches, I saw a guy who was very good-looking, in my opinion. The place where he took his selfie looked so much like my own place *(I have built a house in New England style)* that I was staring at the picture in amazement. The fireplace, globes, and bookshelves looked so familiar to me. It was exactly my style, and so was the way he was dressed.

He said that he loved to exercise and eat healthily. I never even thought about praying for that, but I am extremely conscious of my diet, so I was delighted. When I looked at the date that told me the last time he was online, I became greatly discouraged. *"He looks like the perfect match for me, but of course, he has found somebody already. He wasn't online for more than a year,"* I said aloud to myself. I clicked through a few more pages, lost interest, and decided to go to bed.

However, before I did so, I started wondering about myself and put into question if this discouragement could come from God. *"Usually, you always try to believe in the impossible; why are you so discouraged now?"* I thought. *"Because you've been waiting for a long time to find the right person,"* I said to myself. A stubborn resistance opposed the discouragement that was pressing on me because I knew that my God is still able to do exceedingly, abundantly, above all I could ever think, ask or imagine (see Ephesians 3:20)!

leaned forward on my office desk chair and scrolled back to the place where my future husband's profile was. Looking at it again, I could only shake my head, thinking to myself: *"That would be a miracle."* Still hesitant, I clicked the button and sent him a little wink saying out loud, *"Nothing is impossible with God!"* and went to bed.

Absolutely nothing happened for at least six weeks, at least nothing worth talking about. I was receiving emails constantly but was only disappointed. The good-looking man had not even been online one time, so I was sure he had found his soulmate long ago.

One evening—I was spending the day with a very lovely friend who is a pastor's wife—I came home and checked my mobile phone. Standing in the semi-dark in my kitchen, I saw that somebody from the international singles platform had written me a message. Annoyed, I put my finger on the message, ready to clear it without even opening it. Then I took a deep breath and pulled my finger away from the red field that said "Clear." *"My goodness, the good-looking one!"* I said out loud.

Eagerly, I read the message. Nelson was sending me his number, asking me to contact him if I still would be interested. *"You can't look like you have been waiting for him,"* I thought to myself, *"or he will think you're desperate."* So I waited for a day and then answered him, that he could also reach out to me, sending him my number.

But bummer! The message didn't go through. My time of free access came to an end the same day I wanted to answer him. Gosh, that was a disappointment. *"Now they want my money,"* I thought to myself. *"Probably, he will text me exactly one time, and therefore, I have to sign up for a contract that I don't want to have."*

Suspecting that to happen, I didn't do anything but go to bed and pray, asking God for wisdom. That may seem to be a little bit overdone, but you have to understand that I had to take care of the mortgage of my new house and had developed the property around it beautifully; all the furniture was brand new as well. My house looked like a little castle. In fact, many people stopped to take photographs, and all that didn't come for free. After earning a Swiss salary for years, I wasn't used to counting my money like this anymore.

Therefore, since I had the goal to pay off everything as quickly as possible, I became very careful with my money. A few very unexpected costs popped up, too—as they always do on a big project like this—so I was determined that throwing money out of the window would not be an option. Even if it wasn't that much. So, I made up my mind to wait for three days before I would make any decision. However, after one day, I became so anxious, thinking: *"If you don't give it a shot, you could regret this forever."* Leaving my bed, I went up in the dark, walked into my study, and signed up on the platform. Quickly I forwarded my message to Nelson and went back to bed.

After waking up in the morning, I went running through the woods with my dog as I often did. Coming back, I jumped into the bathtub, a routine that I followed summer and winter with great diligence to stay fit and resilient; when I received a voicemail, it was Nelson.

Listening to his melodic voice, I said to myself: *"Gosh, he is really adorable. Even his voice sounds beautiful."* We never stopped talking ever since and eventually got married.

Moving forward in our relationship, I learned that my husband has a lot of relatives in South America, just like me. I always loved the happiness and positive spirit of my relatives from Brazil, and I always loved their music and felt drawn to their spirit of happiness.

Finding someone who would bring both cultures together in one person, the North and South American cultures, did not even cross my mind. But God, who is able to do exceedingly, abundantly above all that we could ever, think, ask or imagine, did it anyway!

Closing this chapter, I want to tell you that there are many ways God can bring you together with the man he has chosen for you. There are singles groups, vacations for singles, dating platforms, etc. When dating online, please follow the process on the platforms carefully and read their dating tips. For safety reasons, I strongly recommend using a dating site that does a background check using a credit card. Any reputable site will have this process in place. That's why they require your credit card details, even if the first few days are for free. They also have terms and regulations on how what photographs you can post, how to date (safety tips), and so on.

But the most important rule to follow is to stay in the right environment, meaning only date among Christians. It is common sense that you don't find a polar bear on a tropical island. Go to the right places; you must go to the right places.

You might want to test a few options and find platforms that fits you best. I am confident that God will guide your every step toward your future husband.

Praying for you to find your husband!

Nadine

Online Christian Dating Platforms:

Here are a few platforms to consider:

https://www.christiancafe.com/international-dating
https://www.christianmingle.com/en-us
https://www.eharmony.com/
https://www.christianconnection.com/
https://www.christiandatingforfree.com/
https://www.fusion101.com/

YOU CAN HELP YOUR SISTERS FIND LOVE AFTER 30

I hope and pray you've been blessed by what you've read on these pages. Most of all, I hope and pray you will soon be rejoicing in the embrace of the man God has for you.

My vision is to see every Christian woman who desires a husband to be blissfully happy in marriage…and, in the meantime, to enjoy actively engaging in the process of preparation, rather than passively waiting.

One of the most powerful biblical principles is "sow where you want to go." So be sure to plant a seed in the soil of your future marriage today. Just visit the link below and share your testimony of how God has used this book in your life so far:

Review.ChristiansFindingLoveAfter30.com

Every testimony counts because it tells the Amazon algorithm that this is a helpful book, so they should show it to more people.

It would mean so much to me. And to my wonderful husband, too, because he's the one who had to support me in a lot of things while I hid in my office writing this book for you!

I promise to read every review and to show them all to my handsome husband and say, "See, darling, I told you it would be worth it."

YOUR NEXT STEPS

Your Next Steps Now that you've come to the end of *Finding Love After 30*, you may be wondering what you should do next. Well, I've got some great news for you! Our journey together isn't over. In fact, it's just beginning.

Even though God has blessed me with a husband, he has also blessed me with a heart for every woman who still hasn't met the man God has for her. So it would be an honor to stand with you in prayer, and provide practical support and encouragement.

That's why I've started **The Future Wives Club**. Together, we're building an uplifting, faith-filled online community for single Christian professionals. In addition, I offer private and group coaching. Plus, destination events in spectacular "bucket list" locations in Europe and beyond.

Learn more at www.ChristiansFindingLoveAfter30.com

ACKNOWLEDGMENTS

At this point, I would like to thank my beloved husband Nelson for his patience when I was still working at my desk in the evenings, also on Saturdays, and therefore had no time for him. The idea for this book thrilled him, which gave me even more motivation to write. Thank you for all your love, encouragement and support in administrative questions!

I would also like to thank our dear Aunt Maria, who often invited us to dinner on Friday evenings, a nice reward after many hours of hard cognitive work.

Many thanks to my trusted friends, Jessica Lu PhD and Rev. Dr. Scotty J. Williams, for their willingness to share their thoughts and impressions about my book with me in openness and great detail. Jessica encouraged me to share my personal love story as an encouragement to many Christians. Thank you, Jessica!

Furthermore I want to thank Elaine Allen Lechtreck, Ph.D., Sarah Lenz, Tim Griffith and Gina Smith for reading the first draft of this book and giving me honest feedback on it.

Special thanks to Donna Partow - who has mastered the art of writing on a high level - for her precious advice and good tips, which helped me a lot in many ways!

I would also like to thank my dear friend Susanne Berger, who has hoped, believed, and prayed with me that this new phase of life will become the most blessed one I have ever had! I would also like to thank all the positive voices that encouraged me to work on this book.

Dr. Nadine Vargas,
Stamford, CT

ABOUT THE AUTHOR

Nadine Vargas was born in Germany and worked as a nurse for two years. She then trained to become a specialist teacher in the subjects of computer science, macroeconomics, technology, and sports. She then studied pursued degrees in Protestant theology, German, and sport to become a teacher on a master's level. She worked for many years as a teacher in Zurich, Switzerland, and the Bavaria region of Germany.

She began her writing career a decade ago, as the co-author of textbooks and author of children's books. In addition, she has been heavily involved in the fight against human trafficking and forced prostitution and is an ambassador for International Justice Mission. She was invited to the British Parliament in 2019 because of her fight for human rights.

She holds a Doctor of Philosophy in Social Sciences and a Doctor of Letters in Humanities. Nadine loves exercising, reading, traveling, and writing.

She is happily married to Nelson Vargas, a former American Marine.

Manufactured by Amazon.ca
Bolton, ON